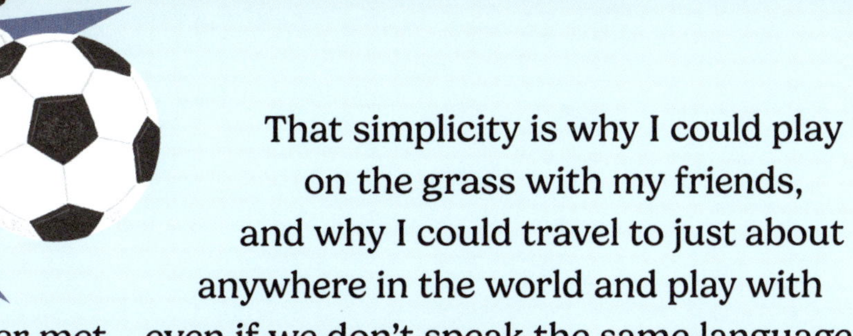

That simplicity is why I could play on the grass with my friends, and why I could travel to just about anywhere in the world and play with people I've never met – even if we don't speak the same language. And you don't need much equipment, which means you don't need a lot of money to play the game. A football pitch brings together people from different backgrounds, and football is the truly global game.

This book introduces some of football's fun and inspiring players, important moments and record-breaking feats. It doesn't cover every word and rule, but it's not supposed to. I hope it can build an interest in the game that might, in time, turn into a love.

S is for Soccer

F is for Football

These different words actually describe the same sport – it really just depends on where you are in the world. Most countries say 'football', while 'soccer' is the preferred term in the United States, Canada and Australia. This is to avoid confusion with other 'football' codes, such as gridiron, Australian rules, rugby union and rugby league.

The interesting thing is that 'soccer' actually originated in Britain and comes from the sport's full name, 'association football', but is rarely used there anymore and is even mocked for cheapening the sport's purity. I prefer 'football' because it represents most of the world's rich history with the sport. But it really doesn't matter what you call it.

A is for

AGUEROOOO!

13 May, 2012: the most memorable day in English Premier League history, when Manchester City snatched a 13th title away from Manchester United's grasp in a split-second of ecstasy and despair (depending on where your loyalty lies). Both teams were on 86 points at the top of the table, though City had an 8-goal advantage. Roberto Mancini's Manchester City had to beat Queens Park Rangers at home, while Alex Ferguson's Manchester United had to beat Sunderland away in order to win the title.

It should have been simple, but a 10-man QPR were somehow 2–1 ahead in stoppage time. Some fans were so tense they had to leave their seats. Others left the ground in tears.

Meanwhile, on the opposite side of the country, United secured a 1–0 win and were seconds away from being crowned champions. Players embraced and awaited their trophy presentation. But then word came that something crazy was happening in Manchester. Edin Džeko had equalised for City in the 92nd minute. The score was 2–2, but City still needed one more goal to claim their first title in 44 years.

In the 94th minute, with seconds to spare, Mario Balotelli spotted Sergio Agüero running into the box and made the perfect pass. Agüero took an equally perfect touch on the ball, cut inside a defender and kicked the goal under immense pressure. He ripped off his shirt and ran, teammates piled on and the stands exploded into pandemonium.

'Aguerooooooo!' cried commentator Martin Tyler, in a clip that became a cultural moment. 'I swear you'll never see anything like this ever again. So watch it, drink it in.'

This finale was the only time a team has won the Premier League on goal difference, and it heralded City's subsequent decade of dominance in the English Premier League.

A is also for ...

Added time

Also known as stoppage time or injury time. These are the extra minutes added to each half by the referee to compensate for time lost during play.

Academy

A training institution that develops young footballers through structured coaching and competition. They often provide a pathway to a professional career for talented players and some are renowned for producing the world's best. Barcelona's academy, La Masia, produced Lionel Messi, Xavi and Andrés Iniesta. Ajax Youth Academy in the Netherlands nurtured Johan Cruyff, Dennis Bergkamp and Frenkie de Jong. And Manchester United Academy gave us David Beckham, Ryan Giggs and Marcus Rashford.

Armband

Worn by a team's captain to distinguish them from the other players. The armband can be any colour, and sometimes they include an image or message to support a cause, such as a rainbow armband for LGBTQ+ rights. Black armbands are worn as a sign of mourning or to commemorate a tragic occasion and are often worn by all players.

Acres of space

A common saying to indicate a player has lots of open area around them and no opponent nearby, allowing them to dribble, pass or shoot without immediate pressure. A term of measurement the US and UK can agree on (even if they can't agree on the name of the actual sport!).

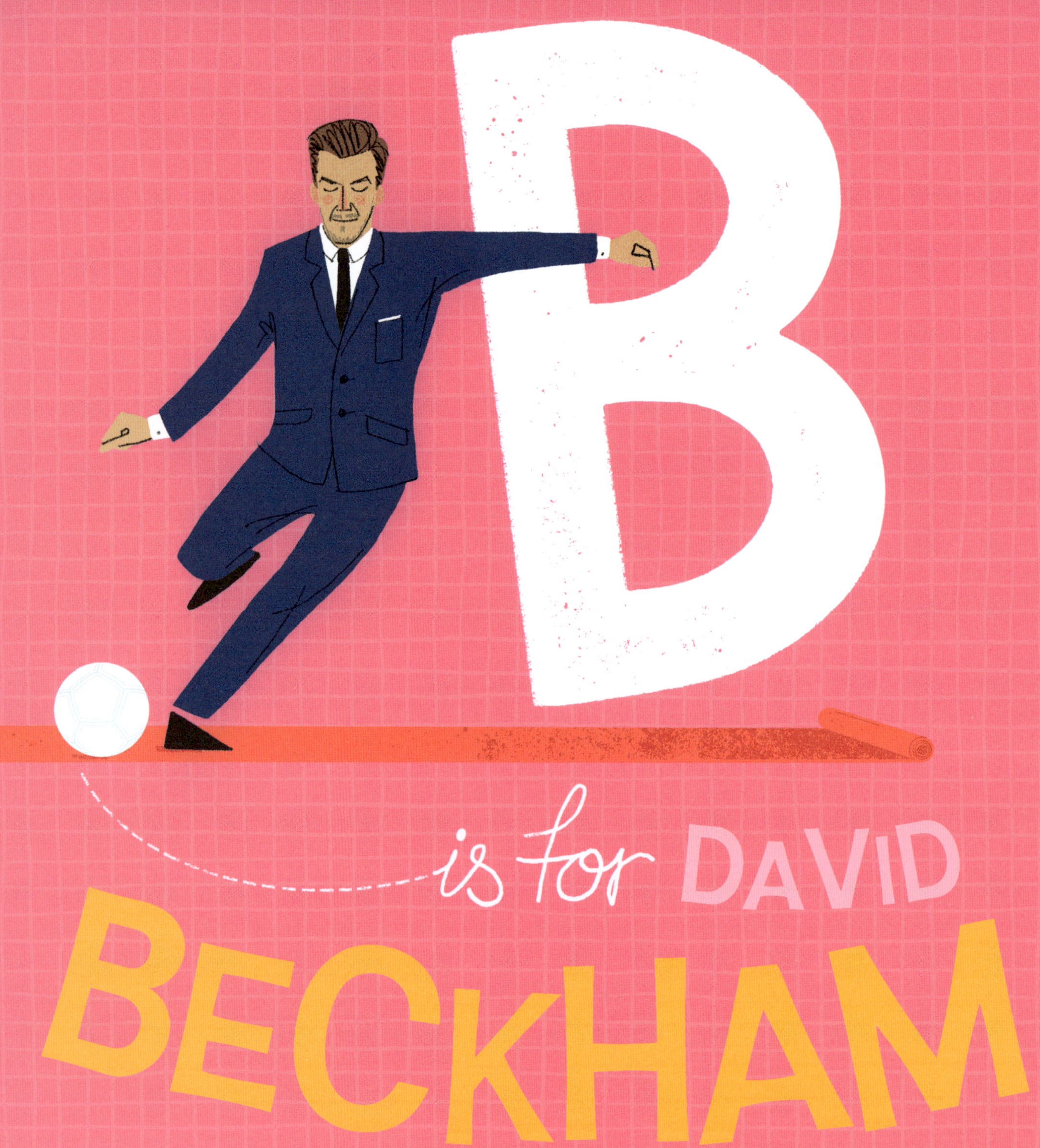

B is for DAVID BECKHAM

David Beckham is one of the world's most recognisable sportspeople, and there are a few reasons why. He was a working-class kid from east London who practised obsessively in the family garden trying to realise his football dreams. His talent most impressed Sir Alex Ferguson, who brought him to Manchester United as a 14-year-old and oversaw his rise to Premier League and Champions League glory.

His free kicks are so flawless they inspired a blockbuster movie (*Bend It Like Beckham*). He played more than 100 games for England, even captaining the Three Lions for several years. And, of course, his marriage to Posh Spice led to them becoming cultural icons. (His many haircuts are also famous in their own right.)

Bicycle kick

An acrobatic strike where a player has their back to the goal and throws their legs over their head while in the air. Also called a scissor kick or overhead kick.

Ballon d'Or

Meaning 'Golden Ball' in French, this award has been given to the best male footballer in the world every year since 1956, as voted by journalists, coaches and national team captains and presented by French magazine *France Football*. Lionel Messi has a record eight awards and Cristiano Ronaldo has five. The Ballon d'Or Féminin has been awarded to the best female footballer since 2018 and been dominated by Spanish stars Alexia Putellas and Aitana Bonmatí.

B is also for ...

Bernabéu

Beckham sometimes sat on the bench at this world-famous Spanish stadium when he was out of favour at its home club, Real Madrid. That was well before the recent renovations that gave the Bernabéu a retractable roof and seating capacity of around 85,000.

Franz Beckenbauer

Widely regarded as the best footballer Germany has ever produced and the most stylish centre-back of all time. Beckenbauer – nicknamed der Kaiser (the Emperor) for his commanding presence, captained West Germany to a World Cup win in 1974 and later managed his country in the 1990 tournament. He also won many trophies with Bayern Munich and was twice awarded the prestigious Ballon d'Or.

Aitana Bonmatí

Bonmatí, like Alexia Putellas, plays for both FC Barcelona and Spain. While she both creates and scores goals, her real influence can be seen in the way she controls the tempo and direction of the ball with smart, unpredictable passes. Bonmatí was at the heart of Spain's 2023 World Cup win and was named player of the tournament, before winning the Ballon d'Or in 2023, 2024 and 2025.

Camp Nou

The colossal home stadium of FC Barcelona since 1957 and a pilgrimage site for football lovers from all over the world. With a capacity of nearly 100,000, it has hosted El Clásicos (matches between Barcelona and Real Madrid), European finals and countless Messi masterclasses. 'Camp Nou' literally means 'new field' in Catalan. In 2023 it closed for major renovations, a lengthy project that Barcelona locals have described as 'like the Sagrada Família taking a day off'.

Johan Cruyff

Dutch master. Revolutionary. Philosopher. Inventor and executer of the iconic Cruyff Turn. Almost single-handedly, Cruyff shaped modern football and his country's footballing reputation, transforming the Netherlands from supporting act to protagonist. He was the face of the Total Football philosophy (see T for more on this), and will be remembered for his rebellious streak as much as his brilliance. 'Football is simple,' Cruyff once said, 'but the hardest thing is to play simple football.'

Chants

Rhythmic songs or shouts from fans in the stands. Chants make the atmosphere feel alive and also intimidate fans of the other team. Sometimes they are serious and heartfelt and other times play with words in a clever, funny way – even to mock teams or players.

'Sacked in the morning, you're getting sacked in the morning'
(to managers, often when their team is playing poorly)

'You don't know what you're doing'
(to referees)

'Que sera, sera / whatever will be, will be / we're going to Wemb-er-ley'
(chant for a team that's headed to a final at Wembley Stadium)

you're getting sacked in the morning...

C is also for ...

Bobby Charlton

The English legend who survived the Munich air disaster of 1958 and went on to win the 1966 World Cup and Ballon d'Or. Admired for his thunderous shooting, Charlton was Manchester United's all-time top-scorer for more than 40 years until his record of 249 goals was surpassed by Wayne Rooney. Beyond football, he embodied fair play and humility, and was never once sent off in his career.

Captain

The player – often older and more experienced – chosen as a team's leader. Also known as the skipper, this person is a motivator, decision-maker and primary link between a squad and manager. On the field they wear the armband and act as mediator with the referee.

Clean sheet

When a team does not concede any goals in a game. Commonly used to judge the performance of goalkeepers and defenders, because they successfully stop the other side from scoring.

Corner kick

When the ball passes over the goal line having last been touched by a player of the defending team, a corner kick is awarded to the attacking team. The kick is taken from the closest corner to where the ball went out, marked by a corner flag. Both teams wait around the goal area to either score or prevent a goal.

Counter-attack

A rapid, direct attack sparked when the defending team wins possession of the ball from an attacking opponent. The players aim to move quickly down the field and score a goal before the opposition can recover their defensive shape after losing the ball.

Cupset

This fun word is a blend of 'cup' (a knockout competition like the FA Cup or Copa del Rey) and 'upset' (a shock result). A cupset happens when a lower-league underdog, often with part-time players, not much money and average facilities, beats a very big, successful club against all odds. A David and Goliath situation.

D is for DRAMA

Late winners. Red cards. Penalty shootouts. Pitch invaders. Few sports offer as many emotional rollercoasters as soccer does – drama is everywhere. It's in the ecstasy of Liverpool's Champions League victory over AC Milan (called the Miracle of Istanbul) in 2005; in Australia's drawn-out, 20-kick penalty-shootout quarter-final win against France in the 2023 Women's World Cup; and in the emotion of Japan's women winning the country's first World Cup mere months after the 2011 earthquake and tsunami.

It is in the Shakespearean tragedy of David Beckham's red card in the 1998 World Cup, and Kylian Mbappé's World Cup final hat-trick – which still didn't save France from losing the final. And in the unsavoury moments: Luis Suárez biting, Zinedine Zidane headbutting and Eric Cantona kung-fu kicking.

Drama keeps us hooked even when we hate it, and has us hugging strangers in the stands when we love it.

Dive

The most theatrical kind of drama where players exaggerate or fake a fall, usually to win a free kick or penalty. A light breeze can hit these players like a freight train, sometimes even causing them to roll around on the ground. But beware: Referees penalise diving.

Dissent

Referees can give yellow cards to players who argue with or challenge their decisions. This backchat is often coupled with sarcastic clapping and expressions of disbelief from the players. Managers are also repeat offenders.

D is also for ...

Dribble

Kicking the ball around the pitch while running at the same time. A successful dribble happens when a player has moved the ball up the field this way and also gotten past a defender. Dribbles can involve tricky outmanoeuvres such as the cut, nutmeg, rivelino, hocus pocus or roulette.

Deadball

When the ball is not actively being played by either team. Examples include free kicks, corner kicks, goal kicks and throw-ins.

Drone

The techy toy coaches often use in training to film their own tactics from above, but occasionally (especially if you are Canada's women's team at the Paris 2024 Olympics) deploy to an opposition training session as a means of spying.

Defender

These players make up the 'back line' of defence as the last layer of protection in front of the goalkeeper. Those positioned in the central area of the pitch are called centre-backs (or centre-halves or central defenders) while those either side are called full-backs (or left-back and right-back). Coaches can play three, four or sometimes even five players as defenders in the back line of defence.

E is for EQUALITY

The past century has been an ebb and flow of progress and setbacks in what was long deemed a 'man's game'. Despite initial inroads in England in the late 19th century (led by Nettie Honeyball), and then a resurgence during the first world war – including a 1920 game (the Dick, Kerr Ladies vs St Helens Ladies) attended by more than 50,000 spectators – the Football Association in 1921 declared football 'quite unsuitable for females' and banned women from playing. Many other countries followed suit, with some medical authorities even claiming that playing could affect a woman's fertility. The FA lifted its prohibition 50 years later, but women still receive far less pay, resources and media coverage than their male counterparts and there are fewer women in leadership roles.

More recently, many players, teams, organisations and fans have started to demand change, like:

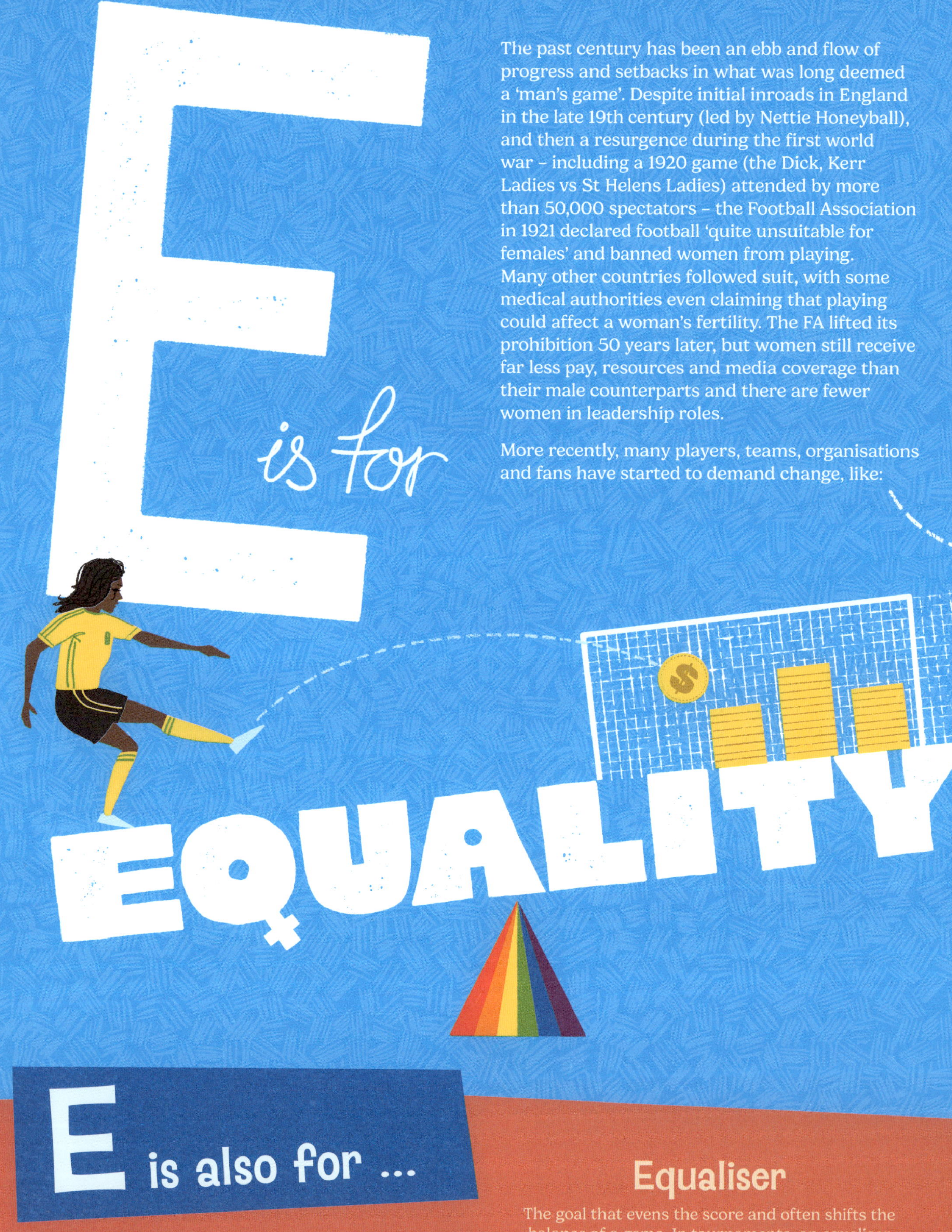

E is also for ...

Equaliser

The goal that evens the score and often shifts the balance of a game. In tournaments, an equaliser scored late in the game can lead to extra time.

Megan Rapinoe

The American Ballon d'Or winner was a leader in the US women's team's high-profile legal fight for equal pay, and has been a highly visible advocate for LGBTQ+ rights, the inclusion of transgender women in women's sports, and against racial injustices. After helping the US get to the 2019 World Cup trophy and herself to the Golden Ball and Golden Boot, Rapinoe used the spotlight to challenge FIFA to invest more in the women's game and increase World Cup prize money.

Nigerian national team

The Super Falcons, Nigeria's national women's team, have staged multiple sit-in protests at their hotel during tournaments, including at the 2019 World Cup, and have staged a training boycott over late or unpaid bonuses and allowances.

Australian national team

Australia's women's team became the first – and only – national sporting team to go on strike in the modern era when in 2015 they refused to tour the US over a pay dispute. The Matildas had just returned home from their most successful World Cup campaign but most were paid less than the national minimum wage. It was a tipping point that heralded their equal pay agreement with the Australian men's team in 2019.

Cedella Marley

The 'fairy godmother' of Jamaica's women's national team (and Bob Marley's daughter). In 2014, after learning the Reggae Girlz had been disbanded in 2008 due to a lack of funding, Marley raised enough money to get the squad back together. Jamaica became the first Caribbean nation to qualify for a Women's World Cup at the 2019 tournament and, in 2023, the first to reach the knockout rounds.

Jenni Hermoso

Spain's 2023 World Cup victory was marred by controversy when football federation president Luis Rubiales forcibly kissed player Jenni Hermoso during the trophy presentation. The incident sparked national and international outrage, leading to protests and renewed demands for accountability, respect and safer environments.

Josh Cavallo

In October 2021, the Australian midfielder for Adelaide United became the first openly gay male top-flight professional footballer in the world. He has since become an advocate for LGBTQ+ equality in sports.

In French FIFA stands for Fédération Internationale de Football Association (or International Federation of Association Football) and is football's world governing body. FIFA was voted into existence in Paris in 1904, with just seven founding member countries: France, Belgium, Spain, Netherlands, Denmark, Sweden and Switzerland. Today, it has a membership of 211 national federations representing countries and territories – from Afghanistan to Zimbabwe – across six continents.

FIFA is like a big umbrella organisation – overseeing the game's development, setting the rules of play, refereeing and coaching standards, and international player transfers. It also organises and promotes – and chooses who gets to host – major football tournaments around the world, including the World Cup. But FIFA has also been accused of corruption, and in 2015 two dozen officials were arrested in Switzerland, prompting a series of reforms designed to increase transparency and accountability within the organisation.

Sir Alex Ferguson

If trophies are the most accurate measure of a manager's success, then 'Fergie' is the best in football history. The Scottish former player has won 49 trophies across his career, including 38 with Manchester United, most notably the club's triple-trophy winning campaign of 1998–99 (he was knighted by the Queen that year). The gum-chewing octogenarian is legendary for nurturing young talent, including the renowned 'Class of '92' featuring David Beckham, Nicky Butt, Ryan Giggs, Gary Neville, Phil Neville and Paul Scholes. He is also famous for coining universally known phrases like 'squeaky-bum time' (the final stages of a close game when either team could win, when squeaking sounds are made by nervous fans squirming on plastic seats), 'it's getting tickly now' and 'football, bloody hell'.

F is also for ...

Foul

Any unfair or dangerous act during play such as tripping, pushing, elbowing or tackling late. Some are tactical, used to disrupt an opponent's attack, while others are just clumsy.

Friendly

A non-competitive match often played as preparation for a tournament or qualifiers. The 'friendly' part is not always followed.

FC

The abbreviation that stands for Football Club and appears in many official team names, even in countries that don't call it football. It sits beside the names of giants and minnows alike, from FC Barcelona to Wrexham AFC (the 'A' is for 'Association').

Full-time

The referee's final whistle to signal the end of the 90 minutes (or stoppage-time of extra time).

Free kick

A free kick is given to a player after a foul. There are two types: direct (you can shoot on the goal) and indirect (you have to pass to another player).

Flick

A quick, clever kick or touch that redirects the ball in some way: to a teammate, over a defender, a backward pass to a player behind or header.

Formation

The arrangement of players on a pitch. Written down this looks like 4-2-2, 4-3-3 or 3-4-3 and shows how many players are in the back, centre and forward line on the pitch. Players are like magnets that can be moved by managers depending on how they want the team to play: with adventure or caution, or something in between.

G is for GOAL!

The aim of the game. How you score one is up to you. You can lace it, curl it, volley it like Zinedine Zidane or backheel it like Alessia Russo. Use your head like Wendie Renard or get fancy with a flick like Neymar. Even a tap-in counts. Sure, it's not as attractive as a dizzying solo run from Maradona, or Messi, or Sam Kerr. But it really doesn't matter, as long as the entire ball crosses over the goal line between the goalposts and under the crossbar. Once that's done, it's time to celebrate. Kerr does a backflip, Messi points to the sky, Ronaldo screams 'siuuuu' and Peter Crouch did the robot dance. Alex Morgan, after scoring for the US against England at the 2019 World Cup, cheekily pretended to sip a cup of tea. Brandi Chastain, after scoring America's World Cup-winning penalty in 1999, swung her shirt around her head in celebration. It was a moment that made her and (and her black sports bra) iconic.

Goal-line technology

A network of sensors, cameras and sometimes magnetic fields to track the ball's position and detect if it has fully crossed the line. This electronic aid provides a signal to the referee when a goal is scored, to help eliminate human error in close calls.

Goalkeeper

Wearing gloves and a different coloured kit to the rest of their team, this position is all about defending the goal. Goalkeepers use techniques such as blocking, smothering, spreading and diving, parrying the ball away or sticking out a foot when needed to make a save. Gianluigi Buffon, Iker Casillas, Mary Earps, Christiane Endler, Manuel Neuer, Hope Solo and Peter Schmeichel have all of these skills and more. They're also the only player allowed to pick up a ball on the field. They're immensely valuable, but can receive little recognition. For example, Soviet player Lev Yashin is the only goalkeeper to have won the Ballon d'Or, having claimed the prestigious award in 1963.

G is also for …

Golden Boot

Awarded to the top-scorer at a major tournament. France's Kylian Mbappé won his Golden Boot at the 2022 FIFA World Cup with eight goals, including a hat-trick against champions Argentina in the final. Japan's Hinata Miyazawa took out the 2023 Women's World Cup Golden Boot honour with five goals.

'Game of two halves'

A cliche used too often to describe a shift in performance or fortune between the first and second halves of a match. The go-to phrase for commentators without something more insightful to say. 'A classic game of two halves, that was. Unfortunately, Team A only showed up for one of them.'

Group of death

In the first part of a tournament, teams are randomly placed into groups, usually of four, and play against each other to determine which ones progress to the next stage. A 'group of death' is a group of teams that are similarly matched and usually strong, making it hard to predict who will succeed. It often leads to chaos.

Do say: 'It's the group of death; one giant's going home early.'

Don't say: 'At least we'll get some match practice in before the tournament proper starts.'

Gaffer

Football (and British) slang for a team's manager or head coach.

H is for

Handball

It's against the rules for the ball and your arm to make contact, which makes sense in a game called football. To decide whether a handball was deliberate, officials take into account the position of the arm to help decide whether a handball was a natural part of a player's movement. In 2019, the International Football Association Board updated its regulations to state that any goal scored directly from a handball – even an accidental one – would be disallowed. The rules have kept evolving since then, and as you can probably guess, everybody is still arguing about it.

Hand of God goal

Back in 1986, during Argentina's World Cup quarter-final with England, Diego Maradona leapt into the air for a header but instead used his left hand to punch the loose ball into the net. The referee did not see it and the goal was allowed. Minutes later, Maradona amazingly dribbled past five England players to score his Goal of the Century and Argentina won 2–1. After the match, Maradona was asked about his first goal and said it was scored 'a little with the head of Maradona, and a little with the hand of God'.

Hairdryer treatment

Sir Alex Ferguson was known for getting a little hot-headed on the pitch. During his time as Manchester United's head coach, the legendary Scot had a tendency to yell at his players so aggressively it felt like a hairdryer blasting in their faces. David Beckham, who was once infamously hit on the head by a flying boot during one of Ferguson's dressing-room rants, said: 'The fear of getting the hairdryer was the reason why we all played so well. He was a manager you wanted to do well for.'

Hat-trick

When a player scores three goals in a single game – they also get to keep the match ball as a souvenir.

H is also for ...

Header

Using the head to control, clear, pass or shoot the ball. France and Lyon captain Wendie Renard is renowned for her power and technique with headers and, despite being a defender, scores many goals with her head.

Hospital pass

You really don't want one of these ill-timed passes from a teammate that's likely to result in you getting tackled and even injured by an opposition player.

Howler

A term to describe the most egregious of errors, both for your team and your reputation. Like scoring an own goal or fumbling an easy save, a howler is a mistake so obvious it's almost comedic. Referees can make them too.

Ada Hegerberg

The first-ever recipient of the Ballon d'Or Féminin, the Norwegian striker also won five consecutive UEFA Women's Champions League titles with her French club Lyon and is the tournament's all-time top-scorer.

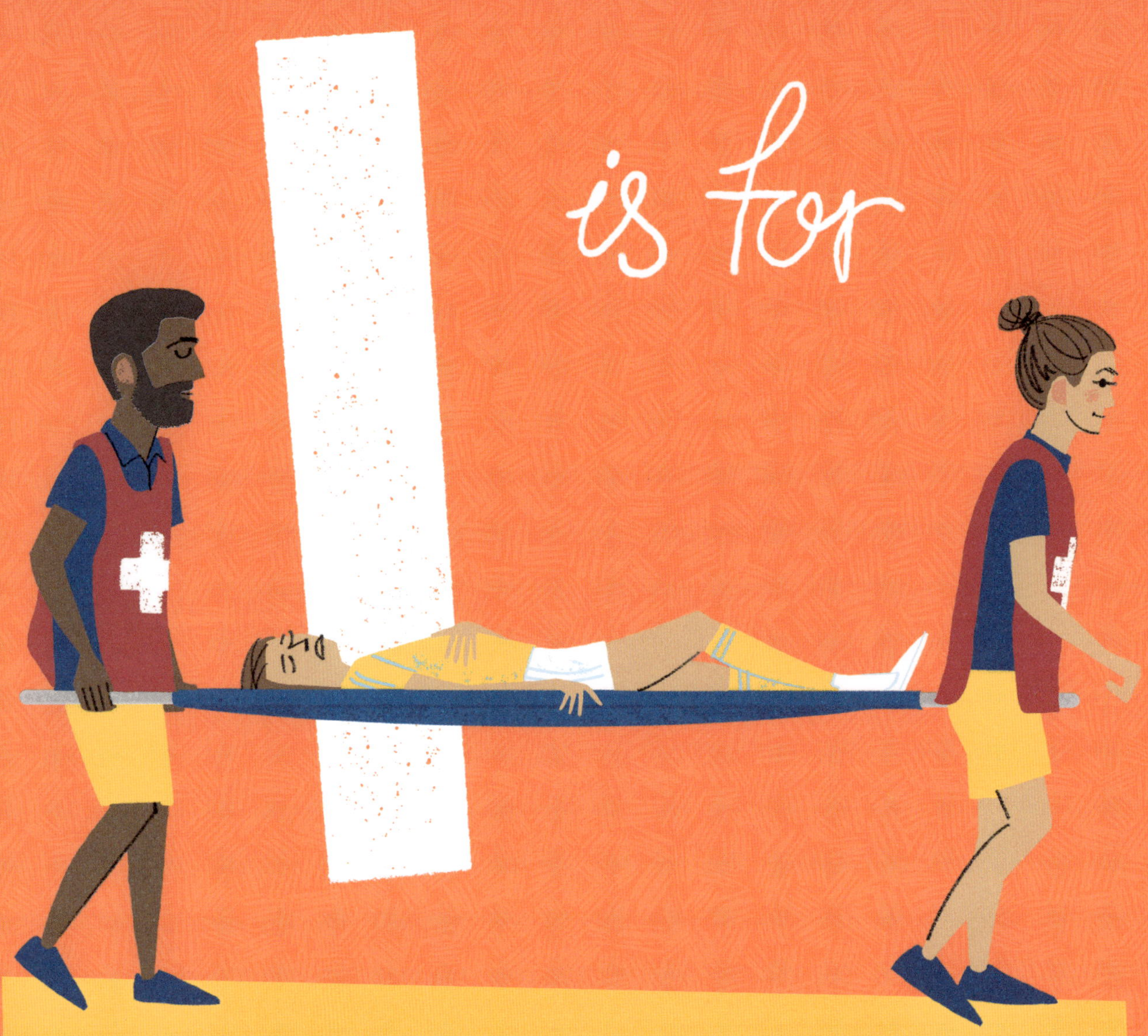

Injuries

Soccer players regularly put their bodies on the line in the pursuit of scoring or defending. Come off on the wrong side of an awkward fall, movement or tackle, and an injury could mean time recovering on the sidelines or even premature retirement. Think hamstring, quad, groin and ankle strains or tears, while a rupture of the anterior cruciate ligament in the knee are especially frequent among women (including Beth Mead, Leah Williamson, Vivianne Miedema and Sam Kerr) and usually mean surgery and up to a year of rehabilitation. Then there's concussion, like the one sustained by Petr Čech in 2006 – the Chelsea goalkeeper suffered a serious collision, resulting in a skull fracture that required emergency surgery. And, of course, there are broken bones. In 2018, Australian winger Hayley Raso fractured three vertebrae in her back after an on-field collision playing for Portland Thorns and re-learned how to walk before miraculously returning to play at the 2019 World Cup.

Inspiration

Beyond the tactics and trophies lie the deeply human stories that move us, on and off the field. Like that of Christian Eriksen, who suffered a cardiac arrest on the pitch during Euro 2020 and would later score for Denmark at the 2022 World Cup. Or the Reggae Girlz, Jamaica's ignored and disbanded women's team who were crowdfunded back into existence by Bob Marley's daughter Cedella and in 2023 became the first Caribbean team to make a World Cup's knockout stages.

Or Nadia Nadim, who fled Afghanistan as a child when the Taliban killed her father. Nadim found refuge in Denmark and went on to become a professional footballer and doctor. English footballer Marcus Rashford's campaign for free school meals in Britain and Sadio Mané's work building hospitals and schools in his native Senegal are two more examples. And who could forget the global effort to rescue a youth football team that was trapped in a cave in Thailand for weeks in 2018? These are just some of the inspirational stories that surround the beautiful game. They remind us how powerful resilience, humility and generosity can be.

I is also for ...

Iceland

This tiny nation with a population of little more than 300,000 qualified for their first-ever major tournament at Euro 2016 and gained a cult following for their fearless play and Viking thunderclap, but most of all because they drew with Portugal, beat Austria with a last-minute goal, and then shocked England 2–1 in the Round of 16 to make the quarter-finals.

Zlatan Ibrahimović

Part striker, part showman, the retired Swedish one-man myth is towering and technical but also endlessly quotable ('I came like a king, left like a legend'). He has a taekwondo black belt that helped him score acrobatic goals from bicycle kicks, volleys and backheels for big clubs like Juventus and Paris Saint-Germain. Pure box office gold.

In their pocket

When a defender has an attacker 'in their pocket', it means they have completely dominated and neutralised the attacker. The ultimate compliment to indicate they have made the attacking player look useless.

The special language of football, from positional and tactical terms such as 'box-to-box midfielder' and 'high press' to slang words like 'nutmeg' and 'gaffer', jargon can sound like another language to uninterested outsiders. We have included some jargon in this book, but there is still plenty more to learn!

Journeyman/journeywoman

A title given to a player who moves between many clubs throughout their career, rarely staying at one long enough to become a meaningful player. Often used in a negative sense, but some players just prefer to move around and experience new things. English former striker Jefferson Louis changed clubs 51 times before retiring.

J is also for ...

Jersey

At first glance they just look like part of the uniform (known as their kit), but football jerseys are actually rich in symbolism about identity and history, and can even be controversial or political. Barcelona's stripes echo the Catalan flag and Germany's white recognises their Prussian heritage, while Italy's Azzurri blue nods to the old royal family. Brazil's canary yellow was not always their colour- they switched after losing the 1950 World Cup in white, convinced that it had brought them bad luck.

Some jerseys have taken on mythical status. Maradona's 1986 World Cup 'Hand of God' kit sold at auction for millions of dollars. Then there's the 1990 West Germany shirt with its bold geometric design, and Nigeria's 2018 zigzag green kit which caused a global frenzy and sold out instantly. Cameroon famously tried sleeveless kits and even a one-piece design, both of which FIFA banned, and Denmark made headlines at the 2022 World Cup for wearing 'protest kits' criticising the human rights record of host nation Qatar.

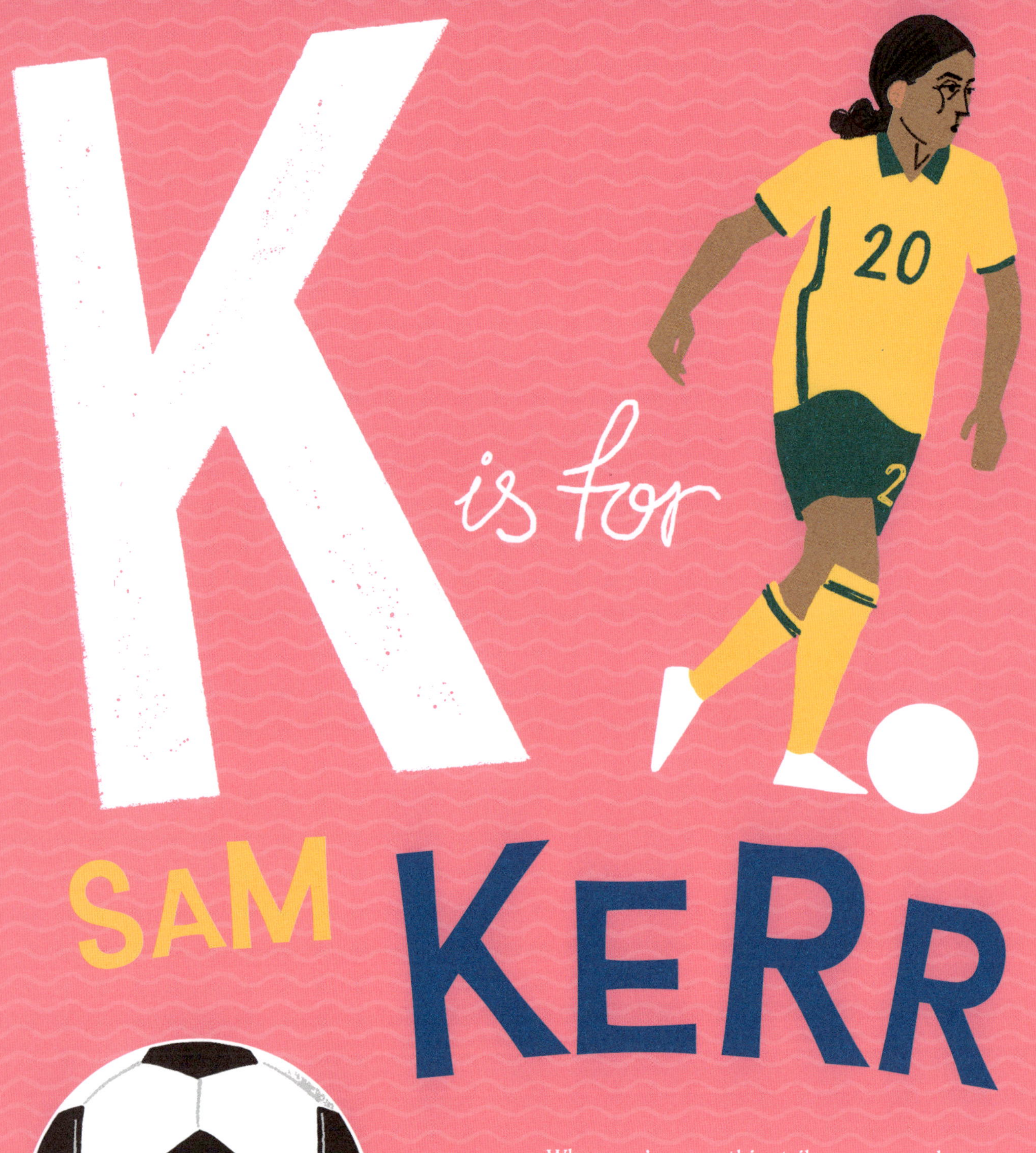

K is for SAM KERR

When you've seen this striker score goals at places like Stamford Bridge and Wembley, it can be hard to remember she was a small-town girl from Perth, Australia, who had to be convinced to give soccer a proper go when a coach spotted her undeniable talent and aerial presence. She debuted for Australia at just 15 and, four World Cups later (including a 2023 home semi-final), is her country's all-time leading scorer. A fan favourite of Australia's women's team the Matildas, she's a star player for Chelsea and is the only player to have won the Golden Boot in three different top-flight leagues.

Kylian Mbappé

As a kid he had posters of Cristiano Ronaldo on his wall, perhaps not realising that he himself was already a star in the making. Mbappé was known as a child in France because of his cool finishing and lightning pace. His sprint speed as an adult has been measured at faster than 38 kilometres per hour (23.6 miles per hour), which is quicker than many Olympic sprinters. Moving at that speed in a game of football looks like you're watching the game on fast-forward. By age 19 Mbappé was helping France win the 2018 World Cup, where he became the first teenager since Pelé to score in a final. There are a few other things that help Mbappé stand out: his trademark folded-arms goal celebration, his charity work and his maturity. As a teenager already in global demand, he declined media interviews to study for his school exams instead.

Keepie-uppie

An addictive everyday pastime also known as juggling or kick-ups. There's one aim: keep the ball off the ground using any part of your body except your hands. Professionals like Brazilian Ronaldinho have turned this dance against gravity into an art form. The world record for keepie-uppie is 28 hours.

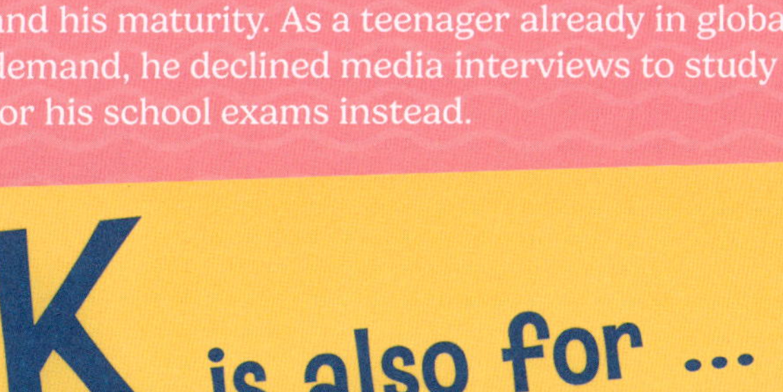

K is also for ...

Edith Klinger

A lesser-known women's football pioneer from Austria, Edith Klinger made her mark not as a player but as the first female referee to officiate both men's and women's games. In the 1930s, women's football in Austria was largely underground and, while not banned outright, dismissed as a novelty. Klinger pushed back on that by taking charge of women's games in Vienna and even men's lower-division matches, where she gained a reputation for fairness and authority. She also organised matches and promoted women's football to help keep it alive during difficult decades in central Europe.

Kill the game

When a team actively prevents the opposition from making a comeback, usually in the form of a match-defining goal that is usually scored in the later stages of the game.

Kick-off

How each half of a match starts, and also restarts after a goal is scored. The ball is placed in the central circle on the field, ready for the initial kick by the team's centre to their teammate, to start play. How the teams approach kick-off is often very strategic, and players will position themselves and move according to a practised plan, which may involve going for a goal straight away or even just stopping the other team from stealing possession of the ball.

L is for THE DICK, KERR LADIES

Ladies on a football pitch were a rare sight until this English team was established during World War I, a time when women filled roles previously held by men, including factory work. This group of women, employed by the Dick, Kerr and Company in Preston, England, played exhibition matches to raise money for injured servicemen. They drew big crowds while defeating similar women's teams across the country, and even represented England internationally during a much-acclaimed tour of France and the United States. On Boxing Day 1920 an estimated 53,000 spectators crammed into Goodison Park to watch their match against St Helens Ladies, with thousands more queued outside. This world-record attendance for a women's match was not broken for almost a century until 2019, when 60,739 packed into Madrid's Metropolitano Stadium to watch Atletico Madrid play Barcelona. The Dick, Kerr Ladies kept playing even after the FA banned women's football in 1921, continuing until 1965 as Preston Ladies FC.

Long ball

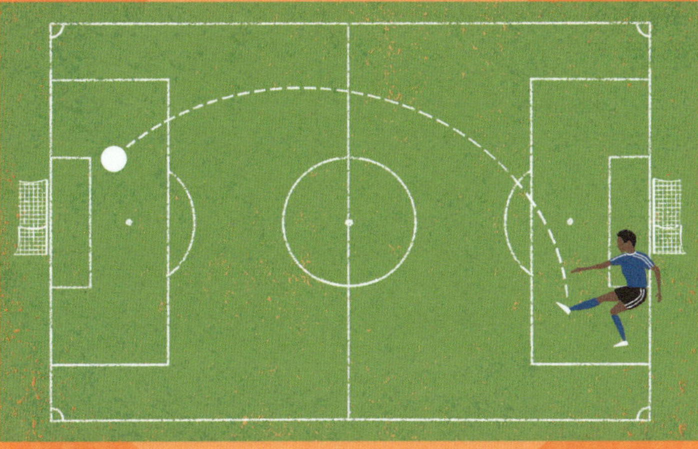

A high, often hopeful pass kicked from deep in defence that travels straight up and over to the other end of the pitch, bypassing the midfield altogether. A long ball is direct and dangerous because it can catch an opponent off guard. But it is also underrated nowadays because many expect football to be more technical and artistic.

Lily Parr

A star player who made her Dick, Kerr Ladies debut at 14 years old, initially as defender at left-back. After moving to the left wing, she quickly became known for her pace, power and aggression, with a reputation for taking corner kicks better than most men and scoring from extraordinary angles. In 2002, Parr, who died aged 73 in 1978, became the first woman to be inducted into the UK's National Football Museum's Hall of Fame, and became immortalised with a statue in the museum in 2019.

L is also for ...

Last man

The final defending player between an attacker and the goal, who is under excruciating pressure to make a well-timed tackle to save the day.

Laws of the Game

The official rules set by International Football Association Board (IFAB) since 1863 with the aim of balancing fairness, flow and safety. The Laws of the Game have been tweaked over time and are often debated, especially interpretations of the handball rule.

Loan

When a player temporarily joins another club, often to gain experience, minutes or a fresh start. Some, like Harry Kane and Ella Toone, use the loan system as a stepping stone to bigger things, while others spend their entire careers bouncing between clubs that are not the one they are signed to play for.

'Lose the dressing room'

When a manager loses the trust, respect or motivation of the players and usually ends up getting fired as a result. This happened to Claudio Ranieri just nine months after the Italian led outsiders Leicester City to a miracle English Premier League title in 2015/16.

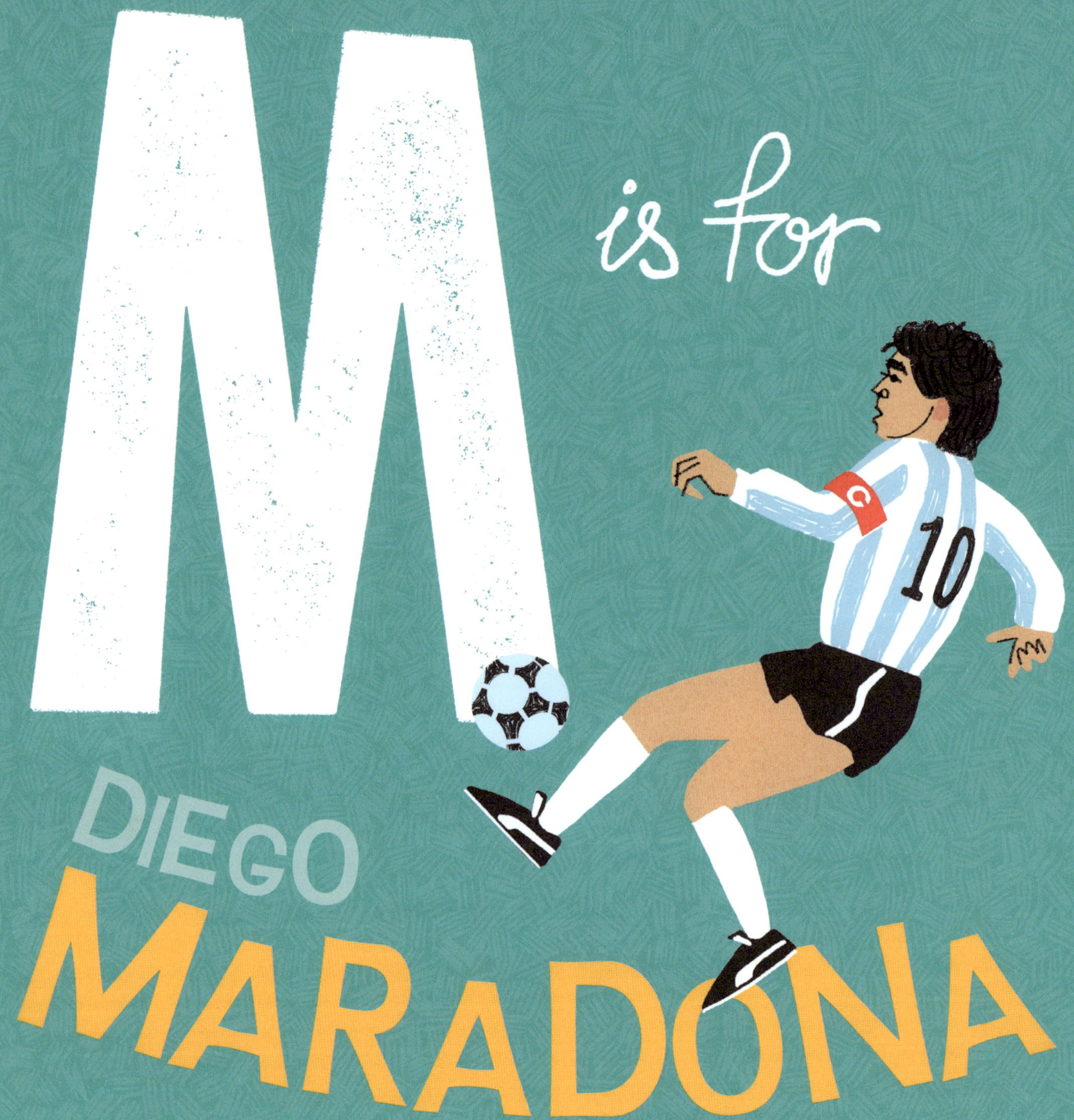

The fabled No.10. The flawed genius himself. They called him El Pelusa (The Fuzz), El Barrilete Cosmico (The Cosmic Kite) and El Cebollita (The Little Onion). Worshipped in his native Argentina for his part in their 1986 World Cup triumph, and in Naples for transforming the unfashionable Napoli into two-time Italian Serie A title champions.

Diego Maradona is iconic as a footballer possessing extraordinary natural talent, and as a larger-than-life personality who defined his generation. Hated as much as he was loved and the source of many BIG FEELINGS, this one complicated man represented so much for so many. When he died in 2020, aged 60, Argentina observed three days of national mourning and almost every game in the world held a minute's silence.

Did you know?

Fans created a parody religion in his name, founding Iglesia Maradoniana (Church of Maradona or Maradonian Church). Complete with Ten Commandments including 'the ball is never soiled' and 'name your first son "Diego"'. Supporters count the years since Maradona's birth in 1960 with the era designation d.D. – 'después de Diego' or 'after Diego'.

He is the most fouled player in World Cup history, having been fouled 53 times throughout the '86 tournament, and also holds the record for a single game (Italy fouled him 23 times at the '82 World Cup).

In 2000, he and Pelé were joint winners of FIFA's Player of the Century award.

Lionel Messi

When Maradona retired in 1997, fans assumed there would never be a player like him again. Until along came one Lionel Messi, another No.10 now widely considered the GOAT (greatest of all time), but nicknamed The Flea. He is, after all, the most decorated footballer in history, with the most Ballons d'Or (eight), almost 50 team trophies, a World Cup win (finally) and more than 850 senior career goals.

M is also for ...

Marta

Once known as 'Pelé in skirts' (with approval from the man himself), Brazil's No.10 is now famous in her own right. As a six-time FIFA women's World Player of the Year. As the all-team leading World Cup scorer, with 17 goals from 23 appearances in six tournaments. And as the first woman to leave her footprints in the Maracanã's hallowed hall of fame. Marta's high profile and longevity have slowly pushed back against the prejudice she says female footballers have always dealt with.

Maracanã

Rio de Janeiro's famous stadium hosted the 1950 and 2014 World Cup finals, with the former – when Uruguay beat Brazil – attended by a record reported crowd of around 200,000. Pelé also scored his 1000th career goal here, in 1969.

Mexican wave

Originating in American football games and popularised internationally during the 1986 FIFA World Cup in Mexico, the universally recognised circuit of standing spectators that travels through the crowd at a packed stadium is known simply as 'the Wave' within North America.

N is for NICKNAMES

A nickname is often bestowed by fans but sometimes by teammates, and generally denotes that a player is either very good or very bad, or has an attribute or name worthy of a bit of fun (maybe even a pun):

Baby-Faced Assassin (Ole Gunnar Solskjaer)

The Butcher of Bilbao (Andoni Goikoetxea)

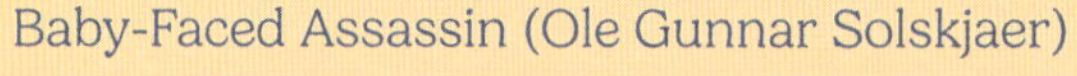

The Divine Ponytail (Roberto Baggio)

Der Kaiser (Franz Beckenbauer)

Bunny (Khadija Shaw)

King (Eric Cantona)

One Size (Fitz Hall)

Dave (Cesar Azpilicueta)

The Black Spider (Lev Yashin)

Uncle (Alyssa Naeher)

Nutmeg

Nope, not the spice used to flavour baked goods, but a dribbling move to beat a defender by kicking the ball between their legs and then retrieving it on the other side.

For Brazilian footballers, it's common to be known by a single name rather than their full, given name, like

Ronaldinho, Marta, Kaká, Formiga, Pelé, Hulk and Neymar.

Teams can also be given nicknames:

Matildas and Socceroos (Australia's women's and men's teams)

The Pharaohs and Cleopatras (Egypt's men's and women's teams)

The Reggae Girlz and Reggae Boyz (Jamaica's women's and men's teams)

N is also for …

Nettie Honeyball

This pioneer formed the first known women's association football club more than a century ago. In 1894, Honeyball placed newspaper adverts seeking young women to join the British Ladies' Football Club. About 30 young women were coached by Tottenham Hotspur player Bill Julian and played their first match the following year at Crouch End in London. Many of the newspapers covering the game remarked on their 'costumes' (loose blouses, knickerbockers or divided skirts, boots and leg pads and a little hat) and concluded it proved women's football was 'totally out of the question'. But this mystery woman, whose name was believed to be a pseudonym, planted a seed that has been growing ever since.

Neymar

Neymar da Silva Santos Júnior is the prodigy who made his professional debut for Santos FC at 17 and soon had the world watching his physics-defying flicks and dribbles, and drawing likenesses to Pelé. His classically Brazilian style, combining individual artistry with innovative team play, continued with European giants Barcelona, whom he helped win the treble (three major trophies in a single season) alongside Lionel Messi and Luis Suárez (the trio nicknamed 'MSN'). Neymar currently has the most international goals of any Brazilian footballer, having surpassed Pelé's previous record of 77 back in 2023.

Shall we get out the salt and pepper shakers to explain? Well, if you insist. If the pepper (attacking player) is closer to the goal than both the salt (defender) and the sauce bottle (the ball) then the pepper is offside. This is only a problem if the pepper is passed the ball by a teammate, because there always has to be a salt shaker between the goal and pepper when the ball is in play.

However, it's worth noting that a player is not considered offside when receiving the ball directly from a throw-in, goal kick or corner kick, or if they are in their own half of the field.

Which parts of the body count as being offside? Any part of the head, body or feet in the wrong position can earn an offside violation but the hands and arms cannot.

is for OFFSIDE

Offside trap

A sneaky, well-timed tactical manoeuvre where defenders – typically the back line – move up the field in unison just as the attacking opponent is about to receive a pass, leaving the attacking player suddenly in an offside position and prompting the referee to call an offside violation.

Old Trafford

Nicknamed 'The Theatre of Dreams' by Bobby Charlton, and rightly so. This historic 74,000-capacity stadium has been home to Manchester United since 1910. It is one of the game's greatest cathedrals where George Best, Eric Cantona and Cristiano Ronaldo achieved legendary status. It's also where 'Fergie time' – the belief that referees gave Alex Ferguson's United extra stoppage-time so they could execute their famed late-game goals – was first granted.

O is also for ...

Olympics

There is a major tournament in women's football every four years as part of the Olympic Games. The US have won a record five times and Brazilian Cristiane is the all-time Olympic top-scorer with 14 goals. The men's tournament is mostly restricted to players under the age of 23, with a limited three spots for older players.

Olimpico

A goal scored when a corner kick curls directly into the net. This spectacular feat, which can happen both deliberately and accidentally, was named after a 1924 goal scored by Argentina's Cesáreo Onzari against reigning Olympic champions Uruguay.

Overlap

A clever move when a defender from the back line runs past a midfield player (who has the ball) on the outside to open up space, often resulting in a cross and attempt at goal. A hallmark of modern attacking full-backs like Lucy Bronze and Trent Alexander-Arnold.

Own goal

The worst possible way to score, it involves kicking the ball into your own net. Often the result of an unlucky deflection, bounce, or a save gone wrong. The stuff of nightmares for players.

'One game at a time'

The ultimate cliche, used by managers and players alike to convey that nothing is guaranteed when asked by the media about their next important match.

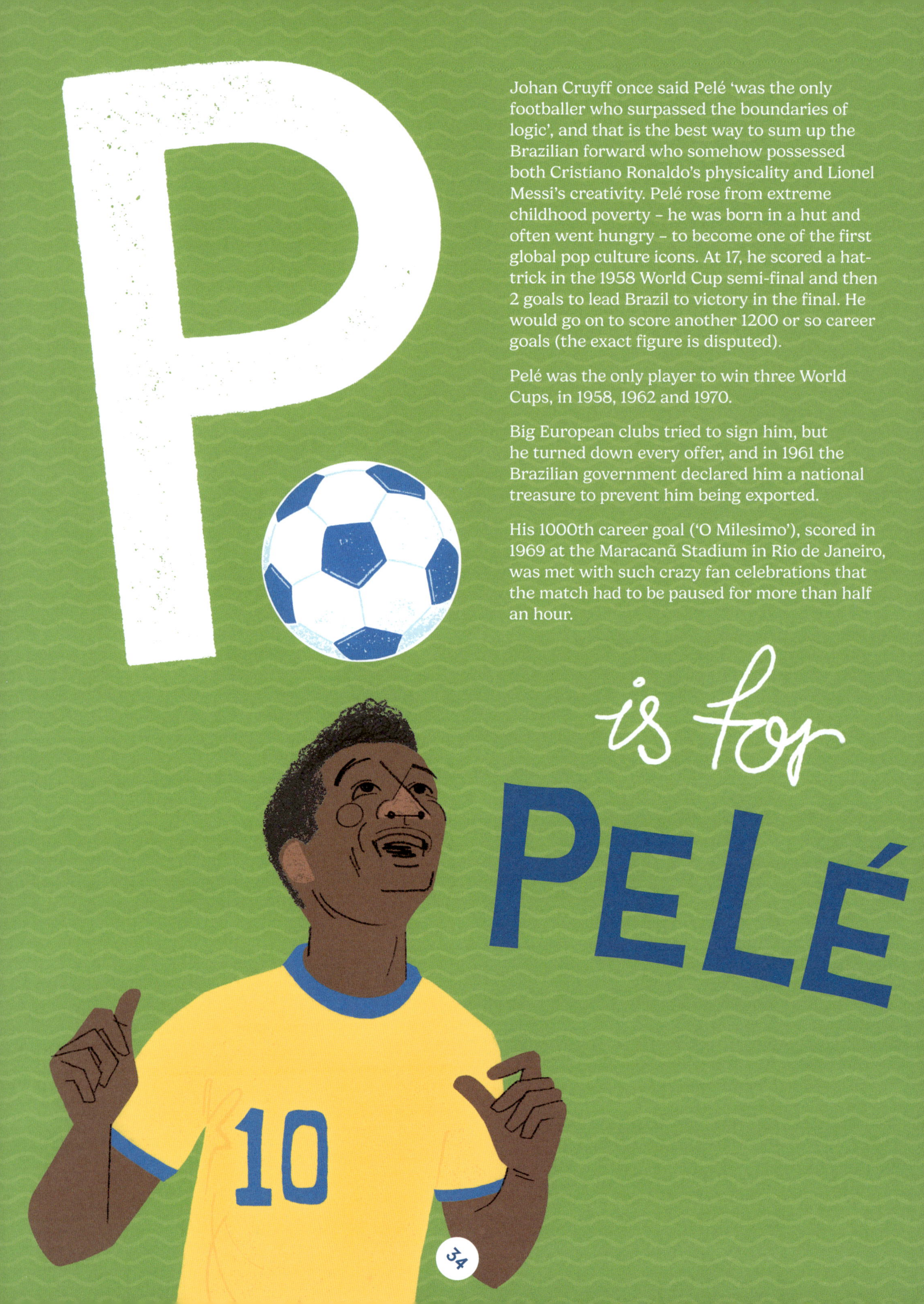

Johan Cruyff once said Pelé 'was the only footballer who surpassed the boundaries of logic', and that is the best way to sum up the Brazilian forward who somehow possessed both Cristiano Ronaldo's physicality and Lionel Messi's creativity. Pelé rose from extreme childhood poverty – he was born in a hut and often went hungry – to become one of the first global pop culture icons. At 17, he scored a hat-trick in the 1958 World Cup semi-final and then 2 goals to lead Brazil to victory in the final. He would go on to score another 1200 or so career goals (the exact figure is disputed).

Pelé was the only player to win three World Cups, in 1958, 1962 and 1970.

Big European clubs tried to sign him, but he turned down every offer, and in 1961 the Brazilian government declared him a national treasure to prevent him being exported.

His 1000th career goal ('O Milesimo'), scored in 1969 at the Maracanã Stadium in Rio de Janeiro, was met with such crazy fan celebrations that the match had to be paused for more than half an hour.

Ferenc Puskás

You may have heard of the Puskás Award, awarded by FIFA for the most beautiful goal each year. Does this offer a hint about what the Hungarian forward was especially good at? That powerful left foot scored a lot, including a double in the 'Match of the Century' of 1953, when Hungary stunned England 6–3 at Wembley Stadium. After the 1956 Hungarian Revolution, Puskás was banned from football for two years for refusing to return home. Once the ban had expired, he joined Real Madrid as an unfit 31-year-old and but went on to play a key role in the club's three European Cups and five La Liga titles. He even became a Spanish citizen and played for Spain at the 1962 World Cup.

Park the bus

An ultra-defensive formation with all 11 players behind the ball. Players in this formation are effectively parking a big bus across the front of the goal to protect a lead or keep out a stronger opponent.

P is also for ...

Penalty shootout

When the score is still level at the end of the game, a penalty shootout is used to decide the winner (for important matches at least). It adds a psychological element that is both brilliant and brutal and can cause even the most composed players to melt under pressure.

Play-off

A knockout match or series of matches to decide qualification for a tournament like the World Cup, or promotion or relegation from a national league.

Ange Postecoglou

A diligent student of Puskás when he coached South Melbourne in Australia, Ange Postecoglou is a trailblazer who has changed European perceptions of Australian football. As manager, he led Celtic FC to multiple trophies before becoming the first Australian to manage in the English Premier League with Tottenham Hotspur.

Panenka

A cheeky type of penalty kick for the confident player who casually shoots the ball down the middle to trick the goalkeeper as they dive to one side or the other. Invented and mastered by Czech player Antonín Panenka in the 1976 European Championship final, this is a risky move that even legendary players can screw up.

Q
is for
QUICK

Footballers can be technically brilliant, have a sharp eye for goal and an amazing football brain, but being quicker than the rest is the key to being unstoppable. Pace and explosiveness are some of the most lethal weapons there are on the pitch, whether you're an attacker running towards goal or starting a counter-attack, or a defender chasing down an opponent. It's why many players incorporate acceleration drills, resistance runs and strength sessions into their training. Kylian Mbappé's top speed of 38 kilometres per hour (or 23.6 miles per hour; recorded in 2019) makes him one of the fastest athletes in any sport, but there is one footballer who is even quicker.

Well, he *was* quicker, because he's retired now, but fellow French star Thierry Henry was recorded running at 39.2 kilometres per hour (24 miles per hour) in 1998. Both of these times are faster than the average speed of Usain Bolt in his 2009 world record (but not Bolt's peak speed of 44.72 kilometres per hour/27.8 miles per hour). The quickest female football player in the world is Zambia's Racheal Kundananji, who reached a top speed of 33.2 kilometres per hour/20.6 miles per hour during the 2023 Women's World Cup.

Q is also for ...

Qualify

To secure a place in the next stage of a competition, whether by finishing high in a league table or surviving the group stage of a tournament. Qualifications for major tournaments can make for exciting stories in their own right, like when Australia's men's team famously beat Uruguay on penalties to qualify for the 2006 World Cup – their first in 32 years. Conversely, the US men's team missed out on qualifying for the first time in 32 years at the hands of Panama, who reached their first ever World Cup in 2018.

Questioning

Players, managers and fans regularly question the decisions of referees, especially if a call goes against their own team and they believe it to be unfair. On the pitch, though, there is a limit. While expressing disagreement in a respectful way can sometimes be okay, repeated arguing, complaining or protesting is classed as dissent, which is misconduct and worthy of punishment such as a yellow card. In community football, many countries use a sin bin – where a player has to sit out, usually for 10 minutes – to discourage abuse of referees.

QUALIFY

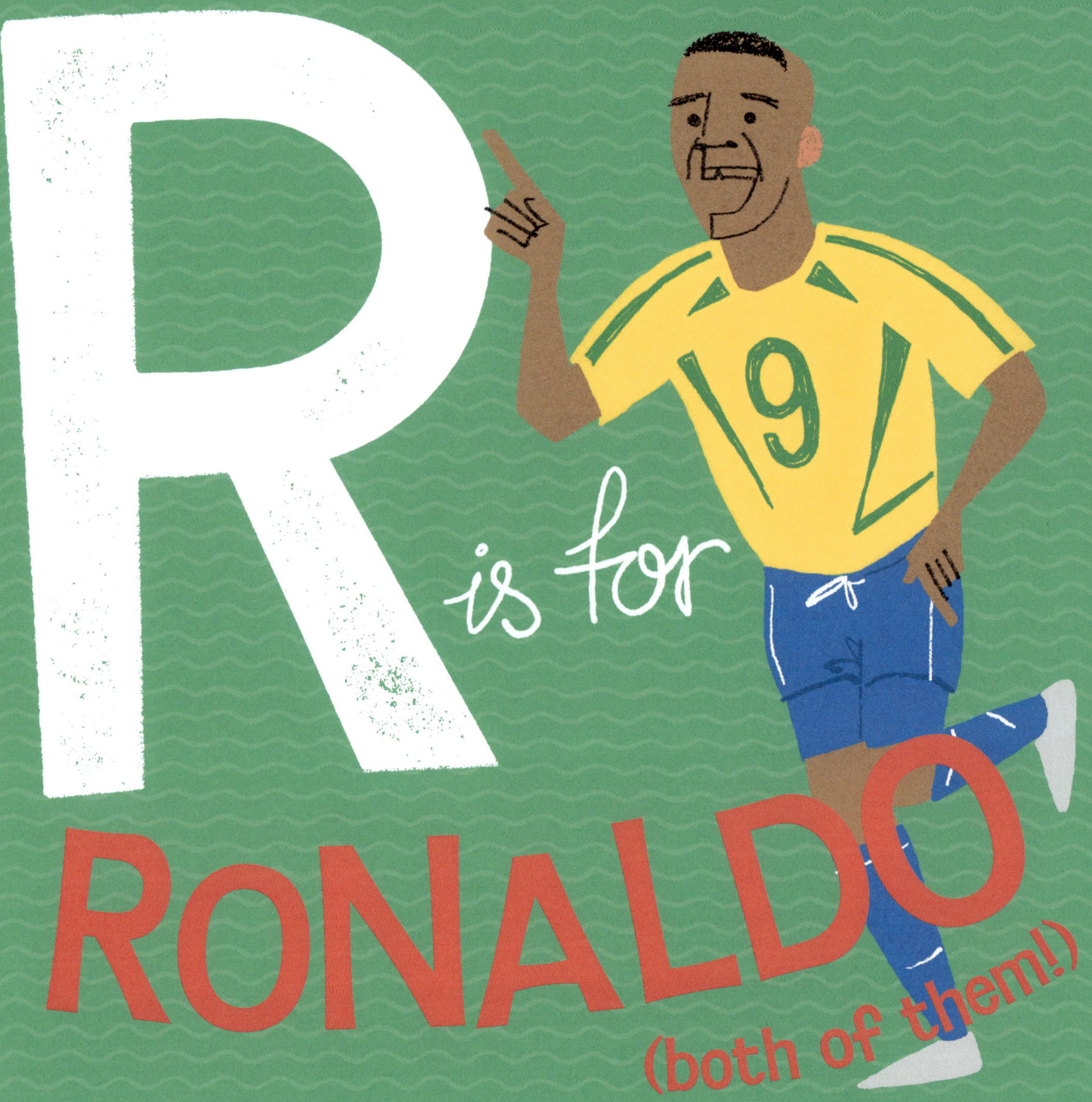

'Original Ronaldo', also known as 'Brazilian Ronaldo', grew up playing football with his friends on the streets and futsal courts of Rio de Janeiro, where he developed the technical skills that turned him into one of the best players ever seen. Ronaldo's upbringing may not have been fancy but his footwork was. By the time he was 20 he had signed with Barcelona and at 21 he became the youngest Ballon d'Or winner. Brazilian fans called him 'O Fenômeno' ('The Phenomenon') because he was somehow able to be everywhere in an instant. Ronaldo managed to score 8 goals in Brazil's 2002 World Cup triumph, and he influenced the next generation of forwards.

One of those forwards is Cristiano Ronaldo. Like his Brazilian idol, the Portuguese forward is renowned for his pace, athleticism and technical skills, and also comes from a poor background. When Sir Alex Ferguson signed the then 18-year-old prodigy he gave him the No.7 shirt already made sacred by George Best, Eric Cantona and David Beckham before him. The nickname CR7 was born, and the rest – the five Ballons d'Or and countless goals and trophies – is history.

Records

Cristiano Ronaldo holds the records for most official goals (933) and most club goals (797).

Christine Sinclair has a record 190 international goals for Canada.

American **Kristine Lilly** is the most-capped footballer to date with 354 appearances for the US over 23 years.

Lionel Messi has the most Ballons d'Or (eight) and goals in a calendar year (91).

Brazil's **Marta** is the World Cup top-scorer with 17 goals (one more than German Miroslav Klose).

Brazil contemporary **Formiga** played at seven different World Cup tournaments.

Pelé is the player with the most World Cups (three for Brazil).

And did you know the **US women's national team** once enjoyed a 44-match unbeaten streak?

Rose Bowl

This stadium in California hosted the 1999 Women's World Cup final, attended by a whopping 90,185 spectators – an international record at the time for a women's sporting event. The United States beat China on penalties, and Brandi Chastain's celebration after her winning spot-kick became one of the sport's most iconic images.

R is also for ...

Referee

The official who controls the game and ensures it is played fairly, safely and according to the rules. If this isn't the case, they can issue a warning or a yellow card, or occasionally even a ...

... Red card

And be sent off immediately. 'Off you hop, Mr Beckham.'

Rivalries

There are some great ones.
Real Madrid v Barcelona (El Clásico)
River Plate v Boca Juniors (Superclásico)
Arsenal v Tottenham Hotspur (North London derby)
Jose Mourinho v The World ('I'm a special one')

Route one

As few passes as possible to get to the goal. Think long and high balls aplenty.

Row Z

Okay, not quite that high. This is the furthest row of seats in the stadium.

S is for STRIKER

A team's main goalscorer, almost always positioned in the final third of the pitch as the attacking focal point for the team, and traditionally wears a No.9 shirt (but not always anymore). Their job: put the ball in the back of the net. Preferably often.

The striker is a more exciting position than many others but also more precarious because worth is judged on statistics, and they are always toeing that painfully fine line between fan favourite and flop depending on whether they are experiencing a 'purple patch' (a run of good luck) or a 'three-game drought' (losing streak).

All strikers live for goals and thrive on service, but there are different kinds:

Target man/woman: a tall, strong and physically imposing player good at winning aerial duels and holding up the ball for teammates to join the attack.
Examples: Abby Wambach, Alan Shearer, Olivier Giroud, Didier Drogba

Poacher: scores goals from close range, often pouncing on loose balls, rebounds and defensive errors inside the penalty area. Has a 'nose for goal' and being in the right place at the right time.
Examples: Gerd Müller, Romário, Gary Lineker, Ruud van Nistelrooy, Sun Wen, Asisat Oshoala

False nine: a centre-forward who, unlike a traditional striker, drops deep into the midfield, pulling defenders out of position.
Examples: Lionel Messi, Francesco Totti, Karim Benzema, Jenni Hermoso, Pernille Harder, Fran Kirby

Complete forward: the most versatile of the lot who has the skills to score goals and create opportunities, often linking up play from the midfield.
Examples: Erling Haaland, Thierry Henry, Harry Kane, Ronaldo, Sam Kerr, Khadija Shaw

S is also for ...

Studs

On the soles of football boots (or soccer cleats) to help players grip the surface, whether that's grass, turf or even mud. Needed for balance and acceleration but can also be dangerous for other players, especially in a studs-up tackle.

Save

When a goalkeeper stops the ball from crossing the goal line using their quick reflexes and good positioning learnt in training. Gordon Banks's save against Pelé's powerful header at the 1970 World Cup is the 'Save of the Century' because of his fantastical explosiveness and flexibility.

Screamer

In football slang, a screamer is a thunderous long-range strike that flies past the goalkeeper with little warning. These goals are celebrated not only for their power but also for their audacity, as the shooter often takes a chance from an improbable distance.

Christine Sinclair

Canada's all-time greatest forward and the world's most prolific international goalscorer – male or female – in history, with more than 190 goals. Known for her leadership and humility, she has played in six FIFA Women's World Cups, scoring in five of them, and captained Canada to Olympic gold in Tokyo 2021.

Spying

Secretly watching an opponent's training sessions to gain tactical insights. Football's real-life James Bond is Argentine manager Marcelo Bielsa. While coaching Leeds United in 2019, he famously admitted to sending staff to watch an upcoming opponent's preparations. It was seen as unethical and became known as 'Spygate'. But Bielsa disagreed, even giving media a detailed presentation on how closely he studies opponents.

Total Football

This philosophy of playing football, invented by Dutch coach Rinus Michels in the 1970s, has revolutionised the way the game is played. Total Football is based on the key principle that no outfield player should have a fixed position. Instead, they are able to swap roles frequently with their teammates to promote a flexible, dynamic unit capable of responding to even the strongest opponents. Elements of Total Football, personified by Dutch great Johan Cruyff with Ajax and Barcelona, are visible in most successful teams today.

is for

Ted Lasso

This cheery character with the big moustache sure did have a lot of belief, but a lot to learn about football! The TV series highlighted the cultural differences between America and Britain, where the earnest, optimistic Ted Lasso coached the struggling AFC Richmond and faced cynical players and brutal fans unaccustomed to his motivational, quirky style.

Tackle

It looks a bit like stealing the ball and running away with it. But a good, clean tackle is a skill that can turn a game by disrupting the attacking team's momentum, and regaining possession of the ball. Achieved either by kicking the ball away or via the more dramatic last-ditch slide, where a defensive player slide kicks the ball away from the attacking player. Be careful not to touch the player before the ball, or go in too hard – or you can expect consequences from the referee.

Tifo

A giant banner held up by fans during a match, created by supporter groups to honour their club, a specific player or a political message. Tifos can be as high or wide as an entire stand, or even made like a mosaic with fans holding separate signs that form one massive picture.

T is also for ...

Tiki-taka

Popularised by Spain's 2010 World Cup-winning team and Barcelona under Pep Guardiola (though he does not like this association), tiki-taka is a tactical style of playing that uses quick, short one-touch passing and intelligent movement of players to maintain possession of the ball. Tiki-taka evolved from the principles of Total Football.

Theme songs

As soon as you walk through the famed Shankly Gates at Anfield stadium in Liverpool, 'You'll Never Walk Alone' becomes a religious hymn. In London, West Ham fans are 'Forever Blowing Bubbles'. And those long-suffering England supporters are still singing 'it's coming home' 60 years after their last major trophy. These unofficial anthems have a way of uniting entire nations and football fans all over the world.

Time

Full time: 90 minutes. A game of two (45 minute) halves. But then there's added time (also called stoppage or injury time) to make up for any time lost during play. If the score is still tied and it's a knockout match, you then have extra time, an additional 30 minutes of play, split into two 15-minute halves. Extra time is intense because both teams know that if neither side scores a winner they will have to go to penalties. Players are weary, making it even more extraordinary when somebody digs deep and finds something special.

Goals in extra time have won World Cup finals, including Andrés Iniesta's 116th-minute winner against the Netherlands to give Spain their first trophy in 2010.

And way back in 1966, when Geoff Hurst scored twice – including a did-it-fully-cross-the-line goal – to complete a hat-trick against West Germany and secure England's only World Cup. The crossbar off which Hurst's highly debated goal bounced is on display at Wembley.

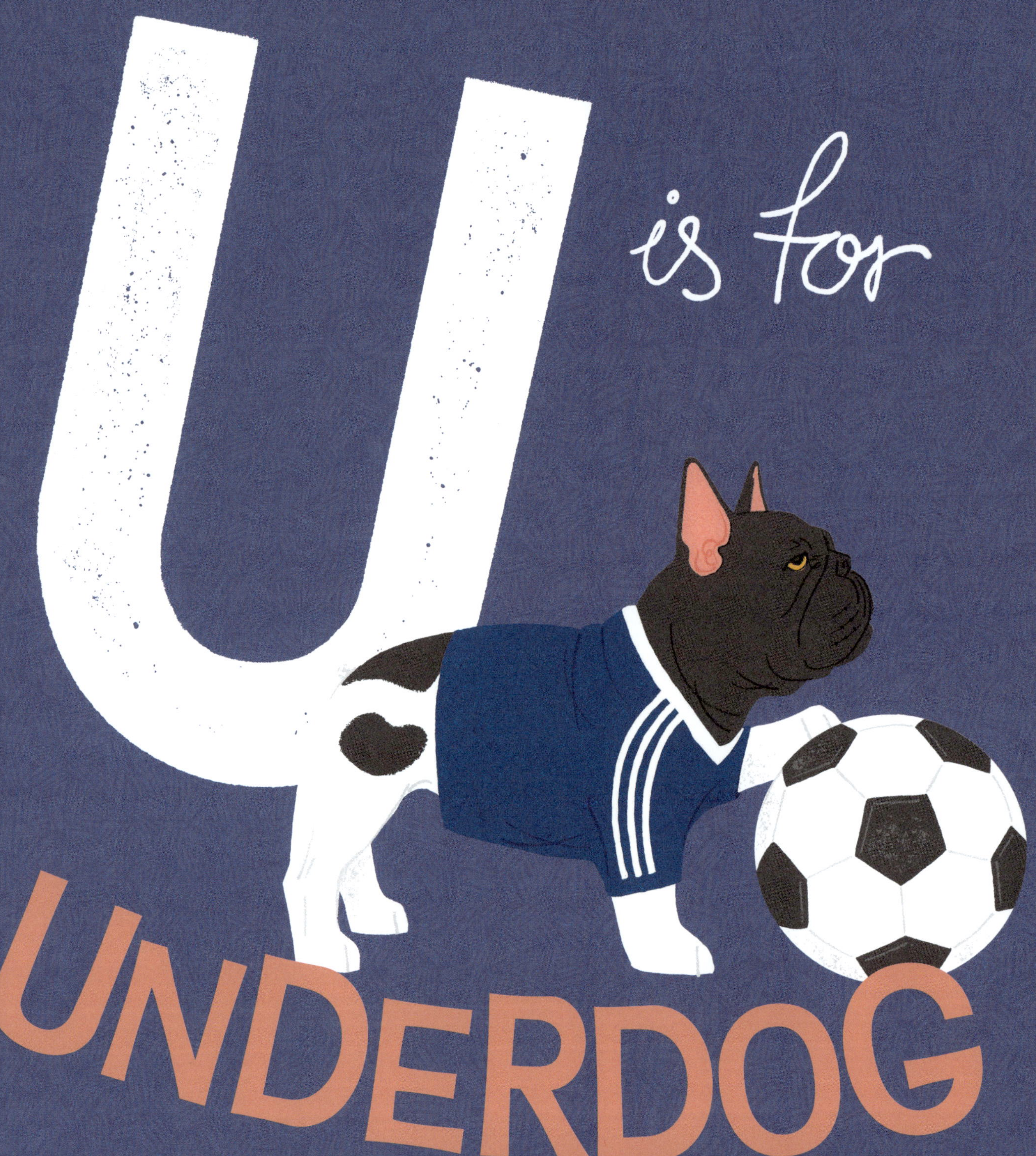

The team we all can't help but cheer for, this is the team not expected to win because the odds are not in their favour, generally due to having fewer star players or fewer wins. The beauty of the underdog lies in the uplifting story, where the little guys overcome adversity and steal the show.

Like Leicester City's against-the-odds Premier League title win in 2015–16, Morocco's remarkable run to the 2022 World Cup semi-finals and Colombia beating Germany to reach the 2023 Women's World Cup quarter-finals.

Urgency

A way to play that maintains a high level of focus and intensity. Ideally, teams aim to play with urgency for an entire match, but often the determination increases as the time remaining decreases – especially if a last-gasp goal is needed for a win or draw.

Ultras

The most vocal and fanatical groups of club supporters known for their chants, organised marches and elaborate displays like tifos and flags and sometimes flares and smoke bombs – bringing the kind of intense atmosphere that makes a stadium feel as if it is vibrating. The term originated in Italy but is now used around the world to identify organised groups of fans. Because of some incidents of violence, a stigma has formed around ultras as groups to be feared.

Unlucky

A word used by players, fans and commentators when a shot bounces off the post, a defender slides in a half-second too late, or a referee misses a foul. Can be used to soften the blow or just reflect that a game hasn't gone your way.

U is also for ...

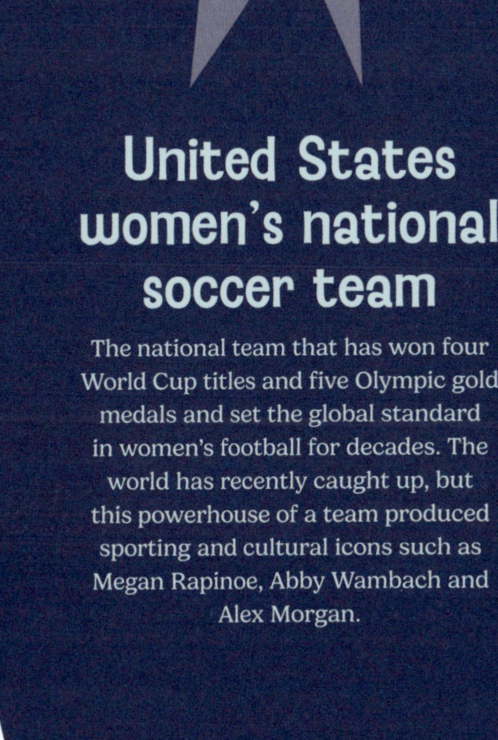

United States women's national soccer team

The national team that has won four World Cup titles and five Olympic gold medals and set the global standard in women's football for decades. The world has recently caught up, but this powerhouse of a team produced sporting and cultural icons such as Megan Rapinoe, Abby Wambach and Alex Morgan.

V is for VAR

Imagine if you could fix all the officiating mistakes ever made and see everything the referee can't. Well, that's what FIFA tried to do when it introduced this new technology in 2018. VAR, which stands for video assistant referee, is a kind of helper for the on-field referee who watches the game on multiple screens inside an operation room. The aim was to increase fairness by reducing 'clear and obvious errors' regarding goals, penalties, red cards and mistaken identity. In reality, VAR has just made the game more controversial, chaotic and complicated, while also sucking the joy out of goal celebrations.

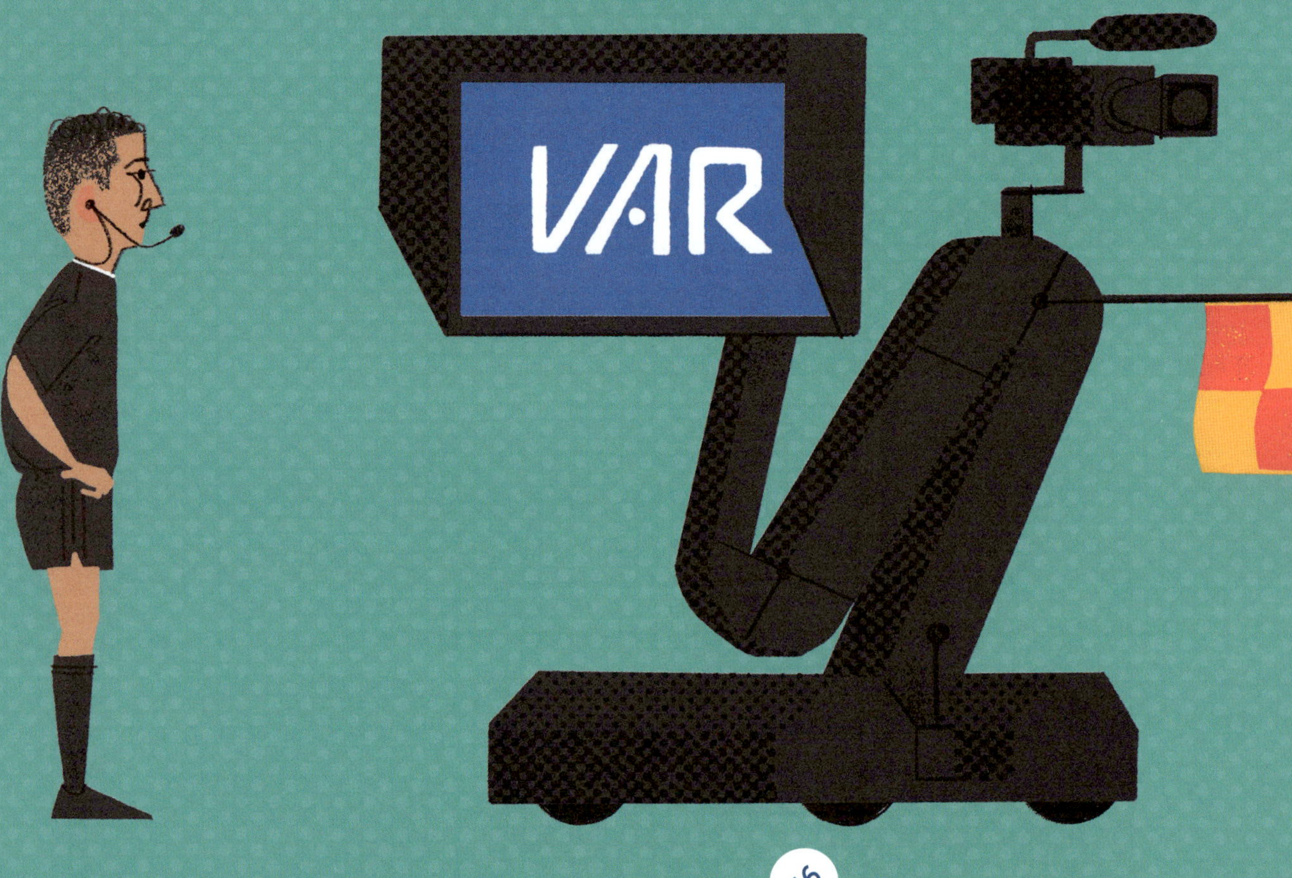

The most famous example was a 2023 English Premier League game, when Liverpool's Luis Díaz had a perfectly good goal against Tottenham wrongly ruled offside on the field. The VAR began a review, but instead of clearing the goal, he mistakenly told the referee the offside call was correct, and Tottenham won 2–1.

In 2018, the VAR system malfunctioned during Australia's A-League Men grand final, right at the moment Melbourne Victory scored a clearly offside goal against Newcastle Jets. By the time the system came back online, it was too late to overturn the goal that ended up being the championship-winner.

Frustrated fans have responded with black humour. Some have cheered and clapped sarcastically every time a referee looks at the screen, and others have made up chants like 'It's not football, it's VAR-ball' and 'VAR my lord, VAR' (to the tune of 'Kumbaya').

Vuvuzela

The defining sound of the 2010 World Cup in South Africa. Believed to have originated in South Africa, the vuvuzela is played by blowing a raspberry into the mouthpiece, and good technique on a good-quality horn will produce a clean sound. However, when hundreds of cheap vuvuzelas are played simultaneously by a bunch of inexperienced football fans, the effect is more like a swarm of insects. The deafening buzz over every match quickly gained international notoriety, and FIFA subsequently banned them from all major tournaments due to the risk of hearing damage, disruption to communication on the pitch and in broadcasts, and general irritation.

V is also for …

Volley

A strike after the ball has been passed or played into the air. A volley requires excellent accuracy and timing from a player, and the capacity to adjust to the ball's trajectory. A volley can also adjust a game's trajectory, like Zinedine Zidane's 2002 European Cup-winning goal for Real Madrid and Marco van Basten's sealer for the Netherlands in the 1988 European Championship final.

Victory

The desired outcome. The opposite of defeat. More simply: a win.

'Viva fútbol'

'Long live football'. Also confirmation the Spanish do not call this game soccer.

Vanishing spray

The magic white foam applied to the pitch to mark the positions for free kicks. It lives inside an aerosol can in a holster on the referee's shorts, makes an appearance when necessary and is gone in 60 seconds. Now you see it …

W is for World Cup

The world's biggest football tournament at which the top national teams compete. The World Cup is held every four years in a different host country. The Men's World Cup began in 1930 and the Women's World Cup started in 1991. Teams first have to qualify by playing against other countries in their region. Then the successful countries start the month-long tournament with a group stage, before moving into the knockout rounds and hopefully reaching the final to determine who becomes world champion.

FIFA WORLD CUP

Did you know?

- Despite almost a century of men's World Cups, there have only ever been eight winners – Brazil, Germany, Italy, Argentina, France, Uruguay, England and Spain. Brazil has the most wins – five.
- Uruguay hosted (and won) the first World Cup. Only 13 teams participated though – many European countries opted against the long and expensive voyage by ship.
- FIFA keeps expanding the men's tournament; from 13 teams to 24 in 1982, 32 teams in 1998 and the 2026 edition will feature 48 teams.
- FIFA did not want to give the World Cup branding to the first women's tournament in 1991, so it was named The First FIFA World Championship for Women's Football, but the public and players still called it the World Cup. It expanded from 12 teams to 16 in 1999, 24 in 2015 and 32 in 2023, showcasing progress of the women's game in countries such as Haiti, Zambia and Vietnam.
- The US have won the women's World Cup four times. Germany, Japan, Norway and Spain have also won.

Wrexham AFC

This Welsh football club was bought in 2020 by actors Ryan Reynolds and Rob McElhenney, who modernised the third-oldest professional football club in the world (it was founded in 1864). All the investment and fan support helped Wrexham rise to League Two in 2023 (the first time in 15 years), and then to League One in 2024, and in 2025 they won their way into the next level up, the Championship.

W is also for ...

Wembley

The London ground is one of the most iconic sports venues in the world, with its distinctive 133-metre-high arch. It's where England won the 1966 World Cup, where every FA Cup is played, and has been the stadium for multiple Champions League and Euro finals (not to mention all the notable concerts). The original stadium, which stood from 1923, was re-opened in 2007 with 90,000 seats. It even has a Royal Box, where winners traditionally walk up the steps to collect their trophies and shake hands with the King.

Abby Wambach

A legend of the game whose international scoring record for the US (184 goals) was surpassed only by Christine Sinclair in 2020 – five years after her retirement. Wambach played at four World Cups (winning in 2015), won two Olympic gold medals and was named FIFA World Player of the Year in 2012, not to mention being an advocate for equality and LGBTQ+ rights.

Worldie

A goal so good, scored with such finesse, that commentators lose their minds and replays are run on repeat, often in slow motion and backed by dramatic music.

That intangible quality you cannot coach. When a certain player seems to operate as if sprinkled with magic dust, sparkling with creativity, charisma or composure and single-handedly turning a game. Arsène Wenger described Thierry Henry in this way, calling him 'a player who could transform a game not just with his feet, but with his imagination'. Messi and Marta are two other obvious candidates here, but there are plenty of others who grab fewer headlines. For example, Nigerian Jay-Jay Okocha and South Korean Ji So-yun are entertainers with a bottomless bag of tricks. Bulgarian Dimitar Berbatov could slow down time with unhurried elegance and Haitian Melchie Dumornay is somehow everywhere and nowhere all at once.

Xavi

Fondly remembered as the midfield metronome for Barcelona and Spain during their tiki-taka era. Xavi always found the right angle for the next pass and could control the rhythm of a game – just like the steady pulse of a metronome helps musicians play in time. Xavi, whose full name is Xavier Hernández Creus, completed a whopping 148 passes in Barcelona's triumphant 2011 Champions League final with a 95 per cent accuracy rate, leaving Manchester United 'passed to death'. It's no surprise, given he joined Barca's world-renowned La Masia academy at age 11 before breaking into the first team at 18. He forged a partnership with fellow players Andrés Iniesta and Sergio Busquets that became the heartbeat of both Barcelona and Spain in their Euro 2008 and 2012, and the 2010 World Cup wins. Lionel Messi called his former Barça teammate, who played more than 500 games for his boyhood club, 'the best player in the history of Spanish football'. After retiring, he returned to Barcelona as a manager and took out the 2022–23 La Liga title.

X is also for ...

X-rated

In football slang, this is a foul, tackle or incident so brutal it is tough to watch and could well earn the player at fault a red card and suspension.

X-ray

A player might have one of these if they are injured on the field and are worried a bone might be broken. An X-ray machine reveals the hidden toll playing and training takes on players' bodies. Some players are also described as having 'X-ray vision' because it seems as if they can see through defences and find a pass or shot not obvious to everybody else.

Y is for

Yard

Even though a football pitch is measured in metres, or metric dimensions, the imperial measurement of a yard (about 0.9 metres) is still in regular use. You might have heard of the 18-yard box (penalty area) and 6-yard box (goal area), and many people still say things like 'she had yards of space' or 'he missed by a yard'.

Yellow card

A formal caution issued by the referee for unsporting behaviour, persistent fouling or arguing with the referee. Two yellow cards in a match means a red card and you're off the pitch for an early shower. One yellow can change a player's style for the rest of the match, and an extra-careful manager may even sub them off to avoid the chance of a red card and being left with only 10 players.

Zero tolerance

A firm stance against racism, sexism, homophobia, transphobia, religious hatred, ableism or any other abuse. Football, being a reflection of wider culture, has endured hundreds of years of problems, and it is only recently that governing bodies, clubs and supporter groups have shown they are serious about making the game safe and inclusive for everyone.

FIFA has implemented anti-racism protocols that allow referees to stop a match if racist chants occur at a stadium.

In England, the Football Association issued lifetime bans and launched an education campaign after homophobic chanting was reported at Wembley during the Women's 2018 FA Cup final. The National Women's Soccer League in America has also banned some fans for life.

In Australia, Sydney FC launched the A-League's first-ever Pride Membership, designed to welcome members of the LGBTQ+ community to the club.

Zinedine Zidane

The French playmaker and World Cup winner known for his elegance, vision and the occasional controversial moment, who later guided Real Madrid to three consecutive Champions League titles as manager. Zizou, as he is popularly known, was born in Marseille to Algerian parents and got his big break at Juventus before moving to Real Madrid and adding more trophies to his growing collection. One was the 2002 Champions League, and his left-footed volley that became the winner is still one of the greatest goals in history. After retiring, he managed Real to three successive Champions League titles from 2016 to 2018 – an achievement unmatched in the modern era. But wait, didn't we forget something? Ah, yes … *that* headbutt during the 2006 World Cup final. Italy's Marco Materazzi came off worse for wear and Zizou got a red card in his last professional match – not the finest way to finish an otherwise terrific career.

A-Z

Academy
Acres of space
Added time
Aguerooo!
Armband
Ballon d'Or
Franz Beckenbauer
David Beckham
Bernabéu
Bicycle kick
Aitana Bonmatí
Camp Nou
Captain
Chants
Bobby Charlton
Clean sheet
Corner kick
Counter-attack
Johan Cruyff
Cupset
Deadball
Defender
Dissent
Dive

Drama
Dribble
Drone
Equaliser
Equality
FC
Sir Alex Ferguson
FIFA
Flick
Formation
Foul
Free kick
Friendly
Full-time
Gaffer
'Game of two halves'
Goal
Goalkeeper
Goal-line technology
Golden Boot
Group of death
Hairdryer treatment
Hand of God goal
Handball

Hat-trick
Header
Ada Hegerberg
Hospital pass
Howler
Zlatan Ibrahimović
Iceland
Injuries
Inspiration
In their pocket
Jargon
Jersey
Journeyman/journeywoman
Keepie-uppie
Sam Kerr
Kick-off
Kill the game
Edith Klinger

Zero tolerance

A firm stance against racism, sexism, homophobia, transphobia, religious hatred, ableism or any other abuse. Football, being a reflection of wider culture, has endured hundreds of years of problems, and it is only recently that governing bodies, clubs and supporter groups have shown they are serious about making the game safe and inclusive for everyone.

FIFA has implemented anti-racism protocols that allow referees to stop a match if racist chants occur at a stadium.

In England, the Football Association issued lifetime bans and launched an education campaign after homophobic chanting was reported at Wembley during the Women's 2018 FA Cup final. The National Women's Soccer League in America has also banned some fans for life.

In Australia, Sydney FC launched the A-League's first-ever Pride Membership, designed to welcome members of the LGBTQ+ community to the club.

Zinedine Zidane

The French playmaker and World Cup winner known for his elegance, vision and the occasional controversial moment, who later guided Real Madrid to three consecutive Champions League titles as manager. Zizou, as he is popularly known, was born in Marseille to Algerian parents and got his big break at Juventus before moving to Real Madrid and adding more trophies to his growing collection. One was the 2002 Champions League, and his left-footed volley that became the winner is still one of the greatest goals in history. After retiring, he managed Real to three successive Champions League titles from 2016 to 2018 – an achievement unmatched in the modern era. But wait, didn't we forget something? Ah, yes … *that* headbutt during the 2006 World Cup final. Italy's Marco Materazzi came off worse for wear and Zizou got a red card in his last professional match – not the finest way to finish an otherwise terrific career.

A-Z

Kylian Mbappé
The Dick, Kerr Ladies
Last man
Laws of the game
Lily Parr
Loan
Long ball
'Lose the dressing room'
Maracanã
Diego Maradona
Marta
Lionel Messi
Mexican wave
Nettie Honeyball
Neymar
Nicknames
Nutmeg
Offside
Offside trap
Old Trafford
Olimpico
Olympics
'One game at a time'
Overlap
Own goal
Panenka
Park the bus
Pelé
Penalty shootout
Play-off
Ange Postecoglou
Ferenc Puskás
Qualify
Questioning
Quick
Records
Red card
Referee
Rivalries
Ronaldo
Rose Bowl
Route one
Row Z
Save
Screamer
Christine Sinclair
Spying
Striker
Studs
Tackle
Ted Lasso
Theme songs
Tifo
Tiki-taka
Time
Total football
Ultras
Underdog
United States women's national soccer team
Unlucky
Urgency
Vanishing spray
VAR
Victory
'Viva fútbol'
Volley
Vuvuzela
Abby Wambach
Wembley
World Cup
Worldie
Wrexham AFC
Xavi
X-factor
X-rated
X-ray
Yard
Yellow card
Zero tolerance
Zinedine Zidane

Published in 2026 by Smith Street Books
Naarm (Melbourne) | Australia
smithstreetbooks.com

Distributed outside of ANZ, North & Latin America by
Thames & Hudson Ltd., 6–24 Britannia Street, London, WC1X 9JD
thamesandhudson.com

EU Authorised Representative: Interart S.A.R.L.
19 rue Charles Auray, 93500 Pantin, Paris, France
productsafety@thameshudson.co.uk; www.interart.fr

ISBN: 978-1-9232-3983-8

Smith Street Books respectfully acknowledges the Wurundjeri People of the Kulin Nation, who are the Traditional Owners of the land on which we work, and we pay our respects to their Elders past and present.

Publisher: Megan Cuthbert
Project editor: Elena Callcott
Editor: Allison Hiew
Illustrator: Nick Radford
Design concept: Andy Warren
Design layout and additional design: Mietta Yans
Proofreader: Ana Jacobsen
Production manager: Aisling Coughlan
Pre-press: Megan Ellis and Andy Warren

Printed & bound in China by C&C Offset Printing Co., Ltd.

Book 442
10 9 8 7 6 5 4 3 2 1